herbs

herbs

fresh aromatic recipes from a country kitchen

LORENZ BOOKS

Published by Lorenz Books
an imprint of
Anness Publishing Limited
Hermes House
88-89 Blackfriars Road
London SE1 8HA

This edition distributed in Canada by Raincoast Books
8680 Cambie Street, Vancouver, British Columbia V6P 6M9

ISBN 0-7548-0095-4

A CIP catalogue record for this book is available from the British Library

Publisher Joanna Lorenz
Senior Cookery Editor Linda Fraser
Assistant Editor Emma Brown
Designers Patrick McLeavey and Jo Brewer
Illustrator Anna Koska
Photographer Michelle Garrett
Recipes Katherine Richmond
Food for photography Liz Trigg
Jacket photography Nicki Dowey

Also published as *The Little Herb Cookbook*

Printed and bound in Singapore

© Anness Publishing Limited 1996, 1999
1 3 5 7 9 10 8 6 4 2

For all recipes, quantities are given in both metric and imperial measures,
and, where appropriate, measures are also given in standard cups and spoons.
Follow one set, but not a mixture, because they are not interchangeable.

Contents

Introduction

One of the most rewarding ways of flavouring food — and giving a familiar dish a unique signature — is by the judicious use of herbs. There's something  very satisfying about stepping outside on a warm summer evening to snip fresh chives, chervil and young sorrel leaves to add to a green salad, or big bunches of parsley for an authentic tabbouleh. Reach for a couple of bay leaves to garnish a terrine or flavour a winter stew and you are instantly transported back to the sunny morning when you picked them and hung them to dry in your kitchen.

Most herbs are easy to grow, demanding little more than a sunny position and light, well-drained soil. Whether you have a garden plot or just a few herbs on the window sill, being able to pick your own herbs and use them instantly, when the essential oils are at their most flavoursome, is richly rewarding. This has been recognized by most supermarkets, which now sell several varieties of growing herbs.

Dried herbs are more pungent than their fresh counterparts. You only need one third to half the quantity. This can be a drawback; dried herbs you seldom use may have lost much of their flavour by the time the jar is empty, so store them carefully, away from direct sunlight, and check the jars often. Throw away any herbs that have become tasteless or musty.

Our ancestors valued herbs highly for medicinal purposes, as a means of flavouring and preserving food, and for their natural beauty and scent. They created beautiful herb gardens, often laid out as wheels or ladders, and hedged with lavender or box. In addition to culinary herbs, they cultivated varieties specifically for their healing properties, to be made into potions, salves or soothing foot baths. Some herbs, such as aniseed and dill seed, were regarded as being good for the digestion. Dill seed was traditionally cooked with cabbage for that reason.

In recent years there has been a resurgence of interest in herbs, both as natural remedies and in cooking. As cooks become more cosmopolitan, herbs like coriander and lemon grass are becoming increasingly popular, and while parsley and mint still hold the high ground, we now expect to be able to buy several varieties of these

familiar herbs, as well as sage, thyme, marjoram, rosemary, oregano, chives and all the other aromatics.

The best way to familiarize yourself with culinary herbs is to be adventurous and to experiment. Although some of the herbs have a natural affinity for certain foods (rosemary with lamb; sage with pork; dill with fish; basil with tomatoes) it is often the unexpected combination that produces the most exciting results. Duck with Red Plums & Coriander, for instance, or Chicken with Blackberries & Lemon Balm are just two of the many delicious recipes that feature in *The Little Herb Cookbook*. From soups, savouries and salads to sweet surprises and refreshing drinks, the book issues an open invitation to explore the wonderful world of culinary herbs.

Kitchen Herbs

BASIL
Known for its affinity with tomatoes, basil is also excellent with fish, pasta and egg dishes.

BAY
The dried leaves are used in stews, soups, casseroles and milk puddings.

CHIVES
Use plain or garlic chives as a garnish for soups and salads, with cream cheese or omelettes.

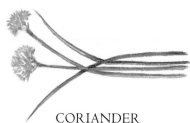

CORIANDER
Try seeds in curries, with roast pork and casseroles. The leaves add a hint of spice to salads, vegetables and some desserts.

DILL
The leaves are used with fish and the seeds for cabbage dishes, marinades and pickles.

MARJORAM
A cultivated variety of oregano, with a milder flavour. Use with lamb, poultry, in stuffings and egg and cheese dishes.

MINT
Don't reserve this refreshing herb for mint sauce. Try it sprinkled over salads, tomato soup or grapefruit.

OREGANO

Although known as the "pizza herb", oregano is not used solely for this purpose. It is widely used in Italian cooking, and goes well with meats, tomatoes, courgettes, eggs and cheese.

PARSLEY

Curly or flat leafed, parsley has a wonderful clean taste. Try it in salads, soups, stuffings and deep fried as a special garnish.

ROSEMARY

The leaves of this pungent herb look like tiny pine needles. Use sparingly in soups, stews or vegetable dishes or insert, with slivers of garlic, in lamb before roasting.

SAGE

These soft, silky grey-green leaves are particularly good with pork, in stuffings (most commonly in combination with onion) and with pan-fried liver.

TARRAGON

Used to flavour vinegar and for fish dishes, sauces (such as Béarnaise, for example) and salad dressings.

THYME

The tiny leaves are widely used in stuffings, meat loaves, tomato dishes and with eggs and cheese.

Techniques

PICKING

Pick herbs often – early in the morning is best. Remove the outer leaves of parsley and chervil first and pick out the tops of basil frequently to stop the plant flowering too early.

DRYING

Herbs are best dried naturally, hung in an airy passageway or kitchen, or laid on a wire rack. They can also be dried overnight in an oven heated to the lowest temperature, then turned off. Strip off the dried leaves from the stems and store whole or crumbled in airtight jars.

10

FREEZING

Chopped or finely snipped tarragon, mint, chives and basil freeze well. Pack them in ice cube trays, fill with water and freeze until solid, then wrap in clear film, label and return to the freezer for up to 6 months.

CHOPPING

Use either a sharp broad-bladed knife or a mezzaluna (a curved blade with a handle at either end) for chopping herbs. The most simple way to chop small amounts of parsley and similar herbs is to put them in a mug and snip using a pair of sharp scissors.

Using Herbs

HERB VINEGAR
See the recipe for Rosemary Vinegar (page 48) for inspiration. Use tarragon, basil or lemon thyme instead of the rosemary, if you prefer.

HERB BUTTER
Top grilled fish or steaks with herb butter: mix 60ml/4 tbsp finely chopped parsley, dill and chervil with 115g/4oz/½ cup softened butter. Shape into a roll, wrap and chill. Cut the butter into slices for serving.

HERB BAKES
Add chopped herbs to scone mixes (see Cheese & Marjoram Scones, page 56), breads or savoury biscuits.

BOUQUET GARNI
Make your own bouquet garni by tying a bay leaf and a sprig each of thyme, marjoram and parsley together.

11

TIME-SAVING TIP
To dry fresh herbs in the microwave, spread the clean sprigs in an even layer between several sheets of kitchen paper and microwave on High (100% power) for 2 minutes. Rearrange the herbs, cover with fresh kitchen paper and cook for about 2 minutes more, checking the herbs every 30 seconds and removing them from the microwave as soon as they appear dry. Leave to cool and dry completely. Never leave the microwave unattended when drying herbs.

Starters &
Light Lunches

Herb & Chilli Gazpacho

INGREDIENTS

1.2kg/ 2½lb ripe tomatoes
2 onions
2 green peppers
1 large cucumber
1 green chilli, seeded
30ml/ 2 tbsp red wine vinegar
15ml/ 1 tbsp balsamic vinegar
30ml/ 2 tbsp olive oil
1 garlic clove, crushed
300ml/ ½ pint/ 1¼ cups tomato juice
30ml/ 2 tbsp tomato purée
30ml/ 2 tbsp chopped mixed fresh herbs, plus
extra to garnish
salt and ground black pepper

SERVES 6

13

1 Set aside about a quarter of the tomatoes, onions, green peppers and cucumber. Roughly chop the remaining vegetables, including the chilli, and place in a food processor or blender. Add the remaining ingredients, with salt and pepper to taste. Process finely, tip into a bowl, then cover and chill.

2 Carefully chop all the reserved vegetables into fine dice and place in a separate bowl for serving with the soup. Alternatively, place the diced vegetables in individual bowls. Serve the soup in chilled bowls, adding one or two crushed ice cubes to each portion. Garnish with herbs.

Pear & Watercress Soup with Stilton Croûtons

INGREDIENTS

1 bunch watercress
4 medium pears, sliced
900ml/1½ pints/3¾ cups chicken stock,
preferably home-made
120ml/4fl oz/½ cup double cream
juice of 1 lime
salt and ground black pepper
CROUTONS
25g/1oz/2 tbsp butter
15ml/1 tbsp olive oil
200g/7oz/3 cups cubed stale bread
150g/5oz/1 cup crumbled Stilton cheese

SERVES 6

14

I Set aside about a third of the water-cress leaves. Place the rest of the watercress leaves and the stalks in a saucepan with the pears, stock and a little salt and pepper. Simmer for 15–20 minutes, until the pears are tender. Transfer the mixture to a food processor or blender. Keeping back some of the reserved watercress leaves for garnishing, add the rest to the pear mixture and immediately process until smooth.

2 Scrape the mixture into a clean saucepan. Stir in the cream and lime juice, mixing thoroughly. Season again to taste. Set the pan aside.

3 To make the croûtons, melt the butter with the oil in a frying pan and fry the bread cubes until golden brown. Drain on kitchen paper. Preheat the grill. Spread the croûtons out in a grill pan, sprinkle the crumbled cheese over the top and heat under a hot grill until bubbling.

4 Reheat the soup over a low heat, stirring occasionally until warmed through. Do not allow the soup to approach boiling point, or it will curdle. Serve in heated bowls, topped with the croûtons and reserved watercress leaves.

COOK'S TIP
The basis of all soups is a good fresh stock, which should be home-made if possible. Stocks can be frozen for up to two months — boil the stock over a high heat to reduce it by half, then cool. Freeze in ice cube trays.

Smoked Trout with Minted Grapefruit

INGREDIENTS

1 lollo rosso lettuce, separated into leaves
15ml/1 tbsp lemon juice
30ml/2 tbsp chopped fresh mint
450g/1lb smoked trout, skinned,
boned and sliced
2 grapefruit, peeled and segmented
120ml/4fl oz/½ cup good bottled
mayonnaise
mint leaves, to garnish

SERVES 4

1 Toss the lettuce leaves with the lemon juice and half the chopped mint in a bowl. Tuck the smoked trout slices among the leaves, then carefully arrange on a serving plate. Add the segments of grapefruit and garnish the salad with mint leaves.

2 Mix the remaining chopped mint with the mayonnaise in a small bowl. Garnish the mayonnaise with two or three mint leaves and serve it with the salad.

VARIATION
Try this alternative for a delicious change. Use smoked mackerel instead of trout and add 15ml/1 tbsp creamed horseradish to the mayonnaise and serve with the salad.

Warm Chicken Salad with Coriander Dressing

INGREDIENTS

4 chicken breasts, boned and skinned
225g/8oz/1½ cups mange-touts
2 heads lollo rosso or feuille de chêne,
separated into leaves
3 carrots, cut into small matchsticks
175g/6oz/1½ cups sliced button mushrooms
6 bacon rashers, grilled and crumbled
15ml/1 tbsp chopped coriander leaves,
to garnish
DRESSING
120ml/4fl oz/½ cup lemon juice
30ml/2 tbsp wholegrain mustard
250ml/8fl oz/1 cup olive oil
75ml/5 tbsp sesame oil
5ml/1 tsp coriander seeds, crushed

SERVES 6

1 Mix together the dressing ingredients. Place the chicken breasts in a shallow dish and pour on half the dressing. Cover the dish and then leave to marinate in a cool place for several hours or chill overnight. Reserve the remaining dressing until required.

2 Cook the mange-touts for 2 minutes in boiling water, then drain, cool under cold running water and pat dry. Arrange the lettuce leaves with the other salad ingredients on serving dishes. Sprinkle with the bacon.

3 Drain the chicken breasts, discarding the dressing used as a marinade. Grill them until cooked through, then slice on the diagonal into quite thin pieces and divide among the portions of salad. Drizzle a little of the reserved dressing over each serving and scatter over some coriander leaves. Serve any remaining dressing separately.

17

Potted Salmon with Lemon & Dill

INGREDIENTS

350g/12oz cooked salmon, skinned
150g/5oz/⅔ cup butter, softened
grated rind and juice of 1 large lemon
10ml/2 tsp chopped fresh dill
75g/3oz/¾ cup flaked almonds,
roughly chopped
salt and ground black pepper
dill sprigs, to garnish
crudités, such as baby corn, fennel wedges,
celery and carrot sticks, to serve

SERVES 6

1 Flake the salmon into a bowl, taking care to remove any bones. Place in a food processor or blender with two-thirds of the butter. Add the lemon rind and juice, half  the chopped fresh dill, and salt and pepper to taste. Process the mixture until quite smooth in texture.

2 Mix in all the flaked almonds. Check for seasoning and adjust if necessary. Scrape the mixture from the food processor or blender into ramekins, levelling  the surface of each with the back of a spoon if you intend to seal the salmon with butter.

3 Seal the potted salmon with butter, if you like: scatter the remaining dill over the top of each ramekin then melt the remaining butter. Set aside until the solids separate then carefully spoon a little of the clarified butter over each ramekin to seal the potted salmon. Chill until set. Garnish with dill sprigs and serve with the crudités.

Normandy Fish with Parsley & Dill

INGREDIENTS

1kg/ 2¼lb white fish fillets
15ml/ 1 tbsp chopped parsley
225g/ 8oz/ 3 cups button mushrooms
225g/ 8oz can tomatoes
475ml/ 16fl oz/ 2 cups cider
10ml/ 2 tsp plain flour
15g/ ½oz/ 1 tbsp butter
1 large bunch dill
45ml/ 3 tbsp Calvados
salt and ground black pepper
parsley leaves, to garnish

SERVES 4

1 Preheat the oven to 180°C/350°F/ Gas 4. Skin the fish carefully with a sharp knife, then chop it roughly and place it in a casserole. Add the chopped parsley, button mushrooms and tomatoes, with the can juices. Season with salt and pepper to taste.

2 Heat the cider in a saucepan to simmering point. Work the flour into the butter to make a paste, then stir it into the cider, a little at a time, making sure that each piece is absorbed before adding the next. Cook, stirring, until the cider has thickened slightly.

3 Set aside a few dill sprigs for the garnish, then chop the rest and stir into the cider mixture with the Calvados. Pour over the fish mixture, cover and bake for about 30 minutes. Serve garnished with the reserved dill sprigs and a few parsley leaves.

Meat & Poultry Dishes

Beef with Herby Orange Mustard

INGREDIENTS

3 oranges
45ml/3 tbsp oil
675g/1½lb braising steak, cubed
2 onions, chopped
1 garlic clove, crushed
30ml/2 tbsp plain flour
300ml/½ pint/1¼ cups beef stock
15ml/1 tbsp tomato purée
45ml/3 tbsp Grand Marnier
15ml/1 tbsp maple syrup
115g/4oz/1 cup sliced mushrooms
30ml/2 tbsp finely chopped mixed fresh herbs,
such as thyme and chives
45ml/3 tbsp Dijon mustard
salt and ground black pepper

SERVES 4

1 Cut one orange in half. Slice one half thinly and set the slices aside. Pare the other 2 oranges very thinly, and cut the pared rind into thin strips. Squeeze the pared oranges and reserve the juice.

2 Preheat the oven to 180°C/350°F/Gas 4. Heat the oil in a flameproof casserole and fry the beef cubes until sealed on all sides. Transfer to a bowl and set aside. Add the onions and garlic to the casserole; fry until softened. Stir in the flour and cook for 1 minute, then gradually stir in the stock.

3 Stir the mixture until it boils and thickens, then return the beef to the casserole and stir in the orange rind strips and orange juice, tomato purée, Grand Marnier and maple syrup. Add salt and pepper to taste. Cover and cook in the oven for about 1½ hours, until the beef is just tender. Add the sliced mushrooms and return the casserole to the oven for 30 minutes more.

4 Meanwhile, grate all the rind from the remaining ½ orange into a bowl. Squeeze in the orange juice. Add the herbs and mustard and mix well. Serve the beef garnished with the reserved orange slices. Offer the herby orange mustard separately. Creamy mashed potato makes an excellent accompaniment.

21

Roast Pork with Sage & Marjoram

INGREDIENTS

2.75kg/6lb leg of pork
45ml/3 tbsp sage leaves
15ml/1 tbsp marjoram leaves
45ml/3 tbsp chopped celery leaves
60ml/4 tbsp cider
salt and ground black pepper
APPLE PUREE
15g/½oz/1 tbsp butter
2 eating apples
2 bananas
15ml/1 tbsp Calvados

SERVES 8

1 Preheat the oven to 180°C/350°F/ Gas 4. Strip off the rind from the pork, leaving an even layer of fat. Cut a piece of foil large enough to enclose the pork and place the pork in the centre. In a bowl, mix the sage, marjoram and celery leaves together. Cover the pork fat with the herb mixture, season to taste and wrap tightly. Support the foil package in a roasting tin (this can be done by placing a wire rack over the tin). Roast for 2 hours.

2 Fold back the foil and drizzle the cider over the pork, taking care not to disturb the herb coating. Continue cooking for 1–1½ hours, until a small sharp knife pressed into the thickest part of the joint produces clear juices.

3 Make the apple purée. Melt the butter in a small saucepan. Peel, quarter and core the apples and slice them into the pan. Turn to coat the slices in butter, then slice the bananas into the pan. Sauté the fruit for 2 minutes. Add the Calvados and set it alight. When the flames die down, remove the mixture from the heat and purée it in a food processor or blender. Spoon the purée into a small jug or bowl and serve with the roast pork.

COOK'S TIP

Herbs are widely used in cooking to add extra flavour to a dish. Although sage and marjoram are classic accompaniments to pork, thyme or rosemary would be equally good.

Lamb Pie with Pear, Ginger & Mint Sauce

INGREDIENTS

1 boned mid-loin of lamb, about 1kg/2¼lb
after boning
15ml/1 tbsp oil
25g/1oz/2 tbsp butter, plus extra for greasing
8 large sheets filo pastry
salt and ground black pepper
flat leaf parsley, to garnish
STUFFING & SAUCE
1 small onion, chopped
15g/½oz/1 tbsp butter
115g/4oz/1 cup wholemeal breadcrumbs
grated rind of 1 lemon
1.5ml/¼ tsp ground ginger
400g/14oz can pears
1 egg, beaten
10ml/2 tsp finely chopped fresh mint, plus
a small sprig, to garnish

SERVES 6

1 Make the stuffing. Fry the onion in the butter until soft. Tip into a bowl and add the breadcrumbs, lemon rind and ginger. Drain the pears, reserving the juice and half the fruit. Chop the remaining pears and add them to the mixture; season and bind with the egg. Spread the loin out flat, fat-side down, and season. Place the stuffing along the middle of the loin and roll up carefully.

2 Holding the meat firmly, close the opening with a trussing needle threaded with string. Heat the oil in heavy frying pan and brown the roll slowly on all sides, until well coloured. Leave to cool, and store in the fridge until needed.

3 Preheat the oven to 200°C/400°F/Gas 6. Melt the butter. Keeping the remainder of the filo covered, brush two sheets with a little butter. Overlap by about 13cm/5in to make a square. Place the next two sheets on top and brush with butter. Continue until the filo has all been used.

4 Remove the string from the lamb and place the roll diagonally across one corner of the pastry, so that it sits within the pastry square, without overhanging the edges. Fold the corner of the pastry over the lamb, fold in the sides, and brush with melted butter. Roll up neatly. Place the roll join-side down on a greased baking sheet and bake for 40 minutes, covering it with foil if it browns too rapidly and looks as if it might burn.

5 Meanwhile, make the sauce. Purée the reserved pears, juice and mint. Pour into a sauce-boat and garnish with a mint sprig. Place the lamb on a platter, garnish with flat leaf parsley and serve with the pear, ginger and mint sauce.

24

Chicken with Blackberries & Lemon Balm

INGREDIENTS

4 chicken breasts, partly boned
25g/1oz/2 tbsp butter
15ml/1 tbsp sunflower oil
60ml/4 tbsp plain flour
150ml/¼ pint/⅔ cup red wine
150ml/¼ pint/⅔ cup chicken stock
grated rind and juice of ½ orange
3 lemon balm sprigs, finely chopped
150ml/¼ pint/⅔ cup double cream
1 egg yolk
115g/4oz/⅔ cup fresh blackberries
salt and ground black pepper
GARNISH
lemon balm sprigs
50g/2oz/⅓ cup fresh blackberries

SERVES 4

1 Preheat the oven to 180°C/350°F/Gas 4. Trim the chicken breasts, removing any skin. Heat the butter and oil in a large frying pan. Fry the chicken until sealed on all sides, then transfer to a casserole.

2 Stir the flour into the fat remaining in the frying pan. Cook for 1 minute, then gradually stir in the wine and stock. Heat, stirring until the sauce thickens. Add the orange rind and juice, and also the chopped lemon balm. Pour over the chicken. Cover the casserole and cook in the oven for 40 minutes.

3 Lightly whisk the cream with the egg yolk in a bowl. Whisk in some of the liquid from the casserole, then stir the contents of the bowl into the casserole. Add

the blackberries. Cover and cook for a further 10–15 minutes. Serve the chicken garnished with the lemon balm and fresh blackberries.

Chicken with Sloe Gin & Juniper

INGREDIENTS

25g/1oz/2 tbsp butter
30ml/2 tbsp sunflower oil
8 chicken breasts, boned and skinned
4 carrots, sliced
1 garlic clove, crushed
15ml/1 tbsp finely chopped parsley
60ml/4 tbsp chicken stock
60ml/4 tbsp red wine
60ml/4 tbsp sloe gin
5ml/1 tsp crushed juniper berries
salt and ground black pepper
shredded fresh basil, to garnish

SERVES 8

27

1 Melt the butter with the oil in a large frying pan. Fry the chicken breasts until they are brown on all sides then transfer to a shallow pan or casserole.

2 Cook the carrots in a saucepan of boiling lightly salted water until tender. Drain and place in a food processor or in a blender. Add the garlic, parsley, stock, wine, gin and juniper berries.

3 Process the carrot mixture to a smooth purée. If the mixture seems too thick, thin it with a little more red wine or water. Pour the sauce over the top of the chicken, then cover and simmer over a low heat for about 15 minutes or until the chicken is cooked through. Season to taste. Transfer to a serving bowl and serve immediately, garnished with shredded fresh basil.

Turkey with Fig & Mint Sauce

28

INGREDIENTS

450g / 1lb dried figs
½ bottle sweet, fruity white wine
15g / ½oz / 1 tbsp butter
4 turkey fillets, 175-225g / 6-8oz each
30ml / 2 tbsp dark orange marmalade
10 mint leaves, chopped
juice of ½ lemon
salt and ground black pepper
mint sprigs, to garnish

SERVES 4

1 Place the figs in a saucepan with the wine. Bring to the boil, lower the heat and simmer very gently for about 1 hour then leave them to cool. Chill overnight.

2 Melt the butter in a frying pan. Fry the turkey fillets until they are cooked right through. Remove them from the pan, cover and keep hot. Drain any fat from the pan and pour in the juice from the figs. Bring to the boil and reduce rapidly until about 150ml/¼ pint/⅔ cup of the juice remains.

3 Add the marmalade to the pan, together with the chopped mint and the lemon juice. Simmer for a few minutes then add salt and pepper to taste.

4 When the sauce is thick and shiny, add the figs and allow to heat through for a couple of minutes, then pour the sauce over the turkey fillets and serve garnished with the mint sprigs.

Duck with Red Plums & Coriander

INGREDIENTS

4 duck breasts, about 175g/6oz each, skinned
10ml/2 tsp crushed stick cinnamon
50g/2oz/¼ cup butter
15ml/1 tbsp plum brandy or Cognac
250ml/8fl oz/1 cup chicken stock
250ml/8fl oz/1 cup double cream
6 red plums, stoned and sliced
6 coriander sprigs, plus extra
to garnish
salt and ground black pepper

SERVES 4

1 Preheat the oven to 190°C/375°F/ Gas 5. Score the duck breasts and sprinkle lightly with salt. Press the crushed cinnamon on both sides of the duck breasts. Melt half the butter in a large frying pan. Fry the duck breasts on both sides to seal, then place them in an ovenproof dish. Pour over the pan juices. Bake for 6–7 minutes. Remove the dish from the oven and return the contents to the cleaned frying pan. Add the brandy and ignite. When the flames die down, remove the duck breasts and keep them hot.

2 Add the stock and cream to the pan and simmer gently until reduced and thickened. Taste the sauce and add more salt and pepper if required.

3 Reserve a few plum slices for the garnish. Melt the remaining butter and fry the plums with the coriander sprigs for just long enough to cook the fruit through.

4 Place the duck breasts on individual plates. Pour a little of the sauce around each portion and divide the plum slices among the plates. Garnish with the coriander and serve at once.

29

Vegetable Dishes & Salads

Vegetable & Herb Kebabs with Green Peppercorn Sauce

INGREDIENTS

16 short or 8 long bamboo skewers, soaked in
water for about 30 minutes
8 flat mushrooms, halved
16 large basil leaves
16 cherry tomatoes
16 large mint leaves
16 chunks of courgette
16 pieces of red pepper
green and purple basil sprigs, to garnish
BASTE
120ml/ 4fl oz/ ½ cup melted butter
1 garlic clove, peeled and crushed
15ml/ 1 tbsp crushed green peppercorns
salt
GREEN PEPPERCORN SAUCE
50g/ 2oz/ ¼ cup butter
45ml/ 3 tbsp brandy
250ml/ 8fl oz/ 1 cup double cream
5ml/ 1 tsp green peppercorns

SERVES 4

31

1 Thread the vegetables on to the bamboo skewers, placing the basil leaves immediately next to the tomatoes, and wrapping the mint leaves around the courgette pieces. Thread on one piece of each type of vegetable per skewer if using short skewers, or two pieces of each per skewer if using long skewers.

2 Preheat the grill. Mix the baste ingredients together in a small bowl and brush over the kebabs so that they are thoroughly moistened. Put the kebabs on a rack and place under the grill. Cook for about 7–8 minutes, turning and basting regularly, until the vegetables are just tender.

3 Meanwhile, make the green peppercorn sauce. Heat the butter in a frying pan, then add the brandy and carefully light it. When the flames die down, stir in the cream and the peppercorns. Cook for about 2 minutes, stirring all the time.

4 When cooked, transfer the kebabs to serving plates and garnish with basil. Serve with the green peppercorn sauce.

Spinach, Walnut & Gruyère Lasagne with Basil

INGREDIENTS

350g/12oz no-need-to-precook
spinach lasagne
30ml/2 tbsp torn basil leaves
15ml/1 tbsp chopped walnuts
WALNUT AND TOMATO SAUCE
45ml/3 tbsp walnut oil
1 large onion, chopped
225g/8oz celeriac, finely chopped
400g/14oz can chopped tomatoes
1 large garlic clove, finely chopped
2.5ml/½ tsp sugar
115g/4oz/1 cup chopped walnuts
150ml/¼ pint/⅔ cup Dubonnet
salt and ground black pepper
SPINACH AND GRUYERE SAUCE
450g/1lb frozen spinach, thawed
75g/3oz/⅓ cup butter
30ml/2 tbsp walnut oil
1 onion, chopped
75g/3oz/¾ cup plain flour
5ml/1 tsp mustard powder
1.2 litres/2 pints/5 cups milk
225g/8oz/2 cups grated Gruyère cheese
grated nutmeg

SERVES 8

1 First make the walnut and tomato sauce. Heat the walnut oil in a saucepan and sauté the onion and celeriac for 8–10 minutes until softened. Meanwhile, purée the tomatoes with their juice in a food processor or blender. Add the garlic to the saucepan and cook for about 1 minute, then add the sugar, chopped walnuts, tomatoes and Dubonnet together with salt and pepper to taste. Simmer, uncovered, for 25 minutes.

2 Preheat the oven to 180°C/350°F/Gas 4. Make the spinach and Gruyère sauce. Purée the spinach. Melt the butter with the walnut oil in a saucepan, add the onion and fry for 5 minutes, then stir in the flour. Cook for 1 minute more, then add the mustard powder and milk, stirring vigorously until the sauce boils and thickens. Remove the pan from the heat and add three-quarters of the grated Gruyère. Stir in the puréed spinach and season to taste with salt, pepper and nutmeg.

3 Spread a layer of the spinach and Gruyère sauce in an ovenproof dish, then add a little walnut and tomato sauce. Top with an even layer of lasagne. Continue layering the sauces and pasta in this way until the dish is full, ending with a layer of sauce. Sprinkle the remaining cheese and the walnuts over the top and strew with basil. Bake for 45 minutes.

Broccoli & Cauliflower with Apple Mint Sauce

INGREDIENTS

4 large apple mint sprigs
30ml / 2 tbsp olive oil
1 large onion, chopped
2 large carrots, chopped
1 large garlic clove, crushed
15ml / 1 tbsp dill seeds
30ml / 2 tbsp plain flour
300ml / ½ pint / 1¼ cups dry cider
450g / 1lb broccoli florets
450g / 1lb cauliflower florets
30ml / 2 tbsp soy sauce
10ml / 2 tsp mint jelly

SERVES 4

34

1 Strip the apple mint leaves from the main stems. Heat the olive oil in a frying pan and sauté the onion, carrots, crushed garlic, dill seeds and mint until the vegetables are almost tender. Stir in the flour and cook for 1 minute, then gradually stir in the cider. Simmer until the sauce looks glossy.

2 Cook the broccoli and cauliflower in separate pans of boiling salted water until tender. Drain, mix together and keep hot in a serving dish. Meanwhile, purée the sauce with the soy sauce and mint jelly in a food processor or blender. Pour the mixture over the broccoli and cauliflower and serve at once.

Courgette & Carrot Ribbons

INGREDIENTS

1 large green pepper, seeded and diced
15ml/1 tbsp sunflower oil
225g/8oz Brie cheese
30ml/2 tbsp crème fraîche
5ml/1 tsp lemon juice
60ml/4 tbsp milk
10ml/2 tsp freshly ground black pepper
30ml/2 tbsp finely chopped parsley,
plus extra to garnish
6 large courgettes
6 large carrots, peeled
salt and ground black pepper

SERVES 4

1 In a saucepan, sauté the green pepper in the oil until just tender. Remove with a slotted spoon and set aside. Process all of the remaining ingredients,

except the courgettes and carrots, in a food processor or blender. Scrape the mixture into the clean saucepan and stir in the green pepper. Set aside.

35

2 Use a vegetable peeler to slice the courgettes and carrots into long, thin strips. Place the courgette strips and carrot strips in separate saucepans, then add water to

cover. Bring to the boil, then lower the heat and simmer for 3 minutes until barely cooked. Drain.

3 Meanwhile, gently heat the green pepper sauce. When hot, pour it into a shallow vegetable dish. Add the courgette and carrot strips to the dish and toss lightly with the sauce until well mixed. Garnish with a little finely chopped parsley and serve the dish at once.

Potato Salad with Rosemary Mayonnaise

INGREDIENTS

1kg/ 2¼lb new potatoes, in skins
pinch of salt
300ml/ ½ pint/ 1¼ cups good
bottled mayonnaise
6 rosemary leaves, finely chopped, plus extra
sprigs to garnish
pinch of black pepper
flat leaf parsley or mixed lettuce, to serve

SERVES 6

36

1 Place the new potatoes in a large saucepan of salted water. Bring to the boil and cook for 15 minutes or until tender. Do not overcook or the potatoes will become mushy and collapse. Drain and tip into a large bowl or colander to cool slightly.

2 Mix the mayonnaise with the chopped rosemary leaves and black pepper to taste. Spoon it over the potatoes while they are still warm and mix together lightly to coat. Leave to cool, then serve on a bed of flat leaf parsley or mixed lettuce leaves, garnished with rosemary sprigs.

COOK'S TIP

For a special treat, use home-made mayonnaise. Place 2 egg yolks in a bowl with a pinch of mustard powder. Very gradually (a few drops at a time) beat in 300ml/ ½ pint/ 1¼ cups vegetable or sunflower oil. If the mayonnaise becomes too thick, add a few drops of lemon juice. Season with salt and white pepper to taste. Mayonnaise can also be made in a food processor or blender — pulse in the oil.

French Bean Salad with Savory

INGREDIENTS

450g/1lb French beans
1kg/2¼lb ripe tomatoes
3 spring onions, roughly sliced
15ml/1 tbsp pine nuts
a few fresh savory sprigs
DRESSING
30ml/2 tbsp extra virgin olive oil
juice of 1 lime
75g/3oz Dolcelatte cheese
1 garlic clove, crushed
salt and ground black pepper

SERVES 4

1 Prepare the dressing first, so that it can stand a while before use. Process the olive oil, lime juice, Dolcelatte and crushed garlic in a food processor or blender until smooth. Pour into a jug or bowl, season to taste and set aside.

2 Top and tail the beans. Cook in a saucepan of boiling salted water until just tender. Drain the beans and rinse under cold running water until cold. (This stops the cooking process and fixes the colour.) Drain on kitchen paper. Slice the tomatoes, or, if they are fairly small, cut them into quarters.

3 Combine all the salad ingredients, except the pine nuts and savory, in a large bowl. Toss together with your hands. Pour the dressing over the top and toss once again, or serve the dressing separately if you prefer. Break the savory into tiny sprigs and sprinkle over the salad, with the pine nuts, just before serving.

37

Desserts & Drinks

Chocolate Mint Truffle Filo Parcels

INGREDIENTS

15ml/1 tbsp very finely chopped mint
75g/3oz/¾ cup ground almonds
50g/2oz plain chocolate
2 eating apples
*115g/4oz/½ cup crème fraîche or
fromage frais*
9 large sheets filo pastry
90ml/6 tbsp melted butter
*15ml/1 tbsp each icing sugar and
cocoa powder, to dust*

MAKES 18

1 Preheat the oven to 190°C/375°F/Gas 5. Grease 2 baking sheets. Mix the mint and almonds in a bowl. Grate in the chocolate. Peel and core the apples and grate them into the bowl too. Stir in the crème fraîche or fromage frais. Cut the filo into eighteen 7.5cm/3in squares, and cover with a clean cloth to prevent them from drying out.

2 Brush a square of filo with melted butter, top with a second square of filo, brush again with butter, then place a spoonful of the filling in the centre. Bring up all  four corners and twist to form a purse shape. Repeat to make approximately 18 filo parcels.

3 Place the filo parcels on the prepared baking sheets. Brush with the remaining melted butter and bake for 10 minutes or until golden. Cool on wire racks, then dust with the icing sugar, followed by the cocoa powder.

Summer Fruit Gâteau with Heartsease

INGREDIENTS

115g/4oz/¹/₂ cup soft margarine,
plus extra for greasing
115g/4oz/¹/₂ cup caster sugar
10ml/2 tsp clear honey
175g/6oz/1¹/₂ cups self-raising flour
2.5ml/¹/₂ tsp baking powder
2 eggs
30-60ml/2-4 tbsp milk
15ml/1 tbsp rose-water
15ml/1 tbsp Cointreau
icing sugar, to dust
450g/1lb/4 cups strawberries
whipped cream or custard sauce,
to serve (optional)
DECORATION
16 heartsease pansies
1 egg white
caster sugar (see method)
strawberry leaves

SERVES 6–8

40

2 Place the soft margarine, sugar, honey, flour, baking powder and eggs in a large mixing bowl. Add 30ml/2 tbsp of the milk and beat well to combine.

Add the rose-water and the Cointreau and mix well. Beat in the remaining milk, if necessary, to give a soft dropping consistency.

3 Pour the mixture into the ring mould and bake for 35–40 minutes or until a skewer inserted in the cake comes out clean. This indicates that it is

cooked. Allow to stand for a few minutes, then turn out on to a serving plate. Leave to cool.

1 Crystallize the heartsease pansies by painting them with lightly beaten egg white, then sprinkling them with caster sugar. Leave on a wire rack to dry. Preheat the oven to 190°C/375°F/Gas 5. Grease and lightly flour an ovenproof ring mould.

4 Sift icing sugar over the cake. Fill the centre with the strawberries and place any extra around the edge. Decorate the serving plate with the crystallized heartsease flowers and some strawberry leaves. Serve the cake cut in thin slices, with whipped cream or custard sauce, if you like.

Iced Lemon Meringue Bombe with Mint Chocolate

INGREDIENTS

2 large lemons
150g/ 5oz/ ⅔ cup sugar
150ml/ ¼ pint/ ⅔ cup whipping cream
600ml/ 1 pint/ 2½ cups Greek yogurt
2 large meringues, lightly crushed
3 mint sprigs
225g/ 8oz good-quality mint chocolate, grated

SERVES 6–8

42

I Pare the lemons thinly, taking care to remove none of the white pith. Chop the pared rind roughly and place it in a food processor or in a blender. Squeeze the lemons and set the juice aside. Add the sugar to the lemon rind and process finely, then add the cream, yogurt and lemon juice and process thoroughly. Pour the mixture into a mixing bowl and add the crushed meringues.

2 Reserve one of the mint sprigs for the decoration; chop the rest finely. Add to the cream and lemon mixture. Pour into a 1.2 litre/2 pint/5 cup bombe mould and freeze for 4 hours.

3 When the ice cream is solid, scoop out the middle and reserve. Set aside a little of the grated mint chocolate for decoration, and tip the rest into the hollow in the ice cream. Fill the hollow with all of the reserved ice cream and return the bombe to the freezer for several hours.

4 To serve, dip the mould in very hot water for a few seconds to loosen the ice cream, then hold a serving plate tightly over the top and invert. Gently remove the mould. Decorate with the reserved grated chocolate and mint sprig and serve immediately.

COOK'S TIP

You can buy ready-made meringue or make your own. To make, whisk 2 egg whites until stiff, whisk in 50g/2oz/¼ cup caster sugar until stiff peaks form, then fold in another 50g/2oz/ ¼ cup caster sugar. Spread out on a baking tray lined with non-stick baking paper and dry in an oven preheated to 150°C/300°F/Gas 2 for about 45 minutes. Allow to cool before using.

Strawberry Punch with Herbs

INGREDIENTS

475ml / 16fl oz / 2 cups clear honey
4 litres / 6¾ pints / 4 US quarts water
475ml / 16fl oz / 2 cups freshly squeezed
lemon juice
45ml / 3 tbsp fresh rosemary leaves,
plus a few sprigs, to decorate
1.5kg / 3½lb / 8 cups sliced strawberries
475ml / 16fl oz / 2 cups freshly squeezed
lime juice
1.75 litres / 3 pints / 7½ cups sparkling
mineral water
ice cubes
3-4 scented geranium leaves

SERVES 30 PLUS

1 Combine the honey and 1 litre/ 1¾ pints/4 cups of the water with 60ml/4 tbsp of the lemon juice in a large saucepan. Add the fresh rosemary leaves. Bring to the boil, stirring until all the honey is dissolved. Remove from the heat and allow to stand until cool. Strain into a large punch bowl.

2 Purée the strawberries by pressing them through a sieve into a bowl using a wooden spoon. Add the purée to the punch bowl with the rest of the water and the citrus juices. Stir gently. Just before serving, pour in the sparkling water, add the ice cubes and float the geranium and rosemary sprigs on the surface.

Citrus Mint Sparkler

INGREDIENTS

4 mint sprigs
2.5ml / ½ tsp sugar
crushed ice
2.5ml / ½ tsp lemon juice
30ml / 2 tbsp grapefruit juice
120ml / 4fl oz / ½ cup chilled tonic water
1 or 2 lemon slices, to decorate

SERVES 1

1 Using a pestle and mortar, crush two of the mint sprigs with the sugar. Scrape the crushed mint into a glass. Fill the glass with crushed ice.

2 Add the lemon juice, grapefruit juice and tonic water. Stir gently and decorate with the remaining mint sprigs and one or two lemon slices.

45

COOK'S TIP

If you prefer, make more than one glass at a time and mix the ingredients in a large jug. For decoration, try freezing tiny sprigs of mint in ice cubes and adding to the drink.

Preserves & Dressings

Dill Pickles

INGREDIENTS

6 small cucumbers
475ml/16fl oz/2 cups water
1 litre/1¾ pints/4 cups white wine vinegar
115g/4oz/½ cup salt
4-6 bay leaves
45ml/3 tbsp dill seeds
2 garlic cloves, slivered
dill flower-heads, to garnish (optional)

MAKES ABOUT 2.5 LITRES/
4 PINTS/2½ US QUARTS

1 Cut the cucumbers diagonally into medium-thick slices and set aside. Put the water, vinegar and salt in a saucepan and bring to the boil. Remove immediately from the heat.

2 Fill sterilized preserving jars with the cucumber slices, tucking the bay leaves, dill seeds and garlic slivers between the layers. Cover with the warm vinegar mixture, filling the jars to the brim.

3 Close the jars tightly and leave on a sunny window sill for at least a week before using. Dill flower-heads can be used to garnish the pickle, if liked.

Rosemary Vinegar

INGREDIENTS

*sufficient rosemary sprigs to fill a 600ml/
1 pint/2½ cup measure, plus extra to decorate
600ml/1 pint/2½ cups white
distilled vinegar*

MAKES ABOUT 600ML/1 PINT/
2½ CUPS

1 Initially, sterilize a wide-necked bottle or pickling jar. Place the rosemary sprigs in the sterilized bottle or jar. Fill to the top with the vinegar. Cover tightly with a suitable lid and place in a sunny spot, such as a window sill, for about 4–6 weeks.

2 Using a coffee filter paper supported in a sieve, filter the vinegar mixture into a saucepan. Discard the rosemary. Heat the vinegar to simmering point but take care not to allow it to boil.

3 If you intend to store the rosemary vinegar in the bottle or jar in which it was made, wash the bottle or jar and its lid well in hot soapy water, rinse thoroughly, and dry in a warm oven. Alternatively, use sterilized decorative bottles. Place a fresh sprig or two of rosemary in the chosen container(s) for decorative purposes, pour in the vinegar, then seal tightly. Store in a dark place and use within 1 year.

Herb Garden Dressing Mix

INGREDIENTS

25g/1oz/1 cup dried oregano
25g/1oz/1 cup dried basil
15g/½oz/½ cup dried marjoram
15g/½oz/½ cup dried dill weed
15g/½oz/½ cup dried mint
60ml/4 tbsp onion powder
30ml/2 tbsp mustard powder
10ml/2 tsp salt
15ml/1 tbsp freshly ground black pepper

MAKES ABOUT 150G/5OZ

1 Mix the ingredients together in a bowl. Transfer the mixture to a clean jar, seal tightly and store in a dry place, out of direct sunlight, until it is required.

2 To make a batch of salad dressing, mix 30ml/2 tbsp of the herb mixture with about 350ml/12fl oz/1½ cups of extra virgin olive oil or sunflower oil and about 120ml/4fl oz/½ cup cider vinegar. Whisk thoroughly. Leave to stand for 1 hour. Whisk again before using.

49

COOK'S TIP
When fresh herbs are not available, this dried herb mixture makes a delicious addition to soups and stews. Try sprinkling it over cooked vegetables, too, for a summery taste.

Rose Petal Jelly

INGREDIENTS

*red or pink roses with sufficient petals
to loosely fill a 600ml/1 pint/
2½ cup measure
475ml/16fl oz/2 cups water
700g/1lb 9oz/generous 3 cups caster or
vanilla sugar
60ml/4 tbsp white grape juice
60ml/4 tbsp red grape juice
50g/2oz powdered fruit pectin
30ml/2 tbsp rose-water*

MAKES ABOUT 900G/2LB

50

1 Remove all the petals from the roses and trim each petal at its base to remove the white tip. Place the rose petals, water and about 75g/3oz/⅓ cup of the sugar in a saucepan and bring to the boil. Reduce the heat and simmer for 5 minutes.

2 Remove the pan from the heat and allow to cool. Cover and leave to stand overnight for the rose fragrance to infuse.

3 Strain the syrup into a large saucepan or preserving pan, and discard the petals. Add the grape juices and pectin and boil hard for 1 minute, then stir in the rest of the sugar until dissolved. Boil the mixture hard for 1 minute more, then remove it from the heat.

4 Test for setting by placing a small spoonful of the hot mixture on a saucer. Leave to cool: the surface should wrinkle when pushed with a finger. If it is still too runny, return to the heat and continue boiling and testing until ready. The consistency should be that of a soft jelly. Alternatively, you can test for setting point using a cooking thermometer – jellies reach setting point at 110°C/225°F.

5 Finally add the rose-water. Ladle the hot jelly into sterilized glass jars and seal at once with waxed paper circles and cellophane lids secured with elastic bands. Decorate the tops of the jars with circles of fabric held in place with lengths of ribbon.

Rhubarb & Ginger Mint Preserve

INGREDIENTS

2kg/4½lb rhubarb
250ml/8fl oz/1 cup water
juice of 1 lemon
5cm/2in piece of fresh root ginger
1.5kg/3lb/6 cups sugar
*115g/4oz/⅔ cup preserved stem
ginger, chopped*
*30-45ml/2-3 tbsp finely chopped mint
(preferably ginger mint) leaves*

MAKES ABOUT 2.75KG/6LB

1 Trim the rhubarb, cutting it into small pieces about 2.5cm/1in in length. Place the rhubarb, water and lemon juice in a preserving pan. Peel and bruise the piece of fresh root ginger. Bring the rhubarb and water to the boil, then add the ginger. Lower the heat and simmer, stirring frequently, until the rhubarb is soft. Remove and discard the ginger.

2 Stir in the sugar until dissolved. Bring to the boil and boil rapidly for 10–15 minutes to reach setting point (see page 50). With a metal slotted spoon, remove any scum from the surface of the preserve.

3 Stir the stem ginger and mint leaves into the cooked preserve, then immediately ladle it into sterilized glass jars. Seal at once with waxed paper circles and cellophane lids secured with elastic bands. Decorate the tops of the jars with circles of brown paper held in place with lengths of raffia.

Dill & Potato Cakes

INGREDIENTS

225g/8oz/2 cups self-raising flour
40g/1½oz/3 tbsp softened butter
pinch of salt
15ml/1 tbsp finely chopped fresh dill
175g/6oz/1 cup freshly made mashed potato
30-45ml/2-3 tbsp milk
dill sprigs, to garnish
butter, to serve

MAKES ABOUT 10

1 Preheat the oven to 230°C/450°F/Gas 8. Grease a baking sheet. Sift the flour into a bowl and add the butter, salt and dill. Now working quickly, add the mashed potato and mix it in with enough of the milk to make a soft pliable dough.

2 Roll out the dough on a lightly floured surface until it is fairly thin. Cut into neat rounds with a 7.5cm/3in cutter. Arrange on the prepared baking sheet and bake for 20–25 minutes until golden. Serve with butter, garnished with dill.

Cheese & Marjoram Scones

INGREDIENTS

115g/4oz/1 cup wholemeal flour
115g/4oz/1 cup self-raising flour
pinch of salt
40g/1½oz/3 tbsp butter, cut into chunks,
plus extra for greasing
1.5ml/¼ tsp mustard powder
10ml/2 tsp dried marjoram
50-75g/2-3oz/½-¾ cup finely grated
Cheddar cheese
milk (see method)
50g/2oz/½ cup chopped pecan nuts
or walnuts
butter, to serve

MAKES ABOUT 18

56

1 Preheat the oven to 220°C/425°F/ Gas 7. Grease 2 large or 3 small baking sheets with butter. Sift the wholemeal and self-raising flours into a bowl and add the salt. Rub the butter into the dry ingredients until the mixture resembles fine breadcrumbs.

2 Mix the mustard powder, dried marjoram and cheese into the butter and flour mixture. Working quickly, mix in sufficient milk to make a soft, not sticky dough. Knead the dough lightly for a few minutes until it is smooth and pliable.

3 Roll out the dough on a floured surface to a thickness of about 2cm/¾in. Using a 5cm/2in square or round cutter, cut out about 18 scones.

4 Brush the scones with a little milk and sprinkle with the chopped nuts. Bake for 12 minutes or until well risen and golden. Serve warm, with butter.

COOK'S TIP

Scones taste better if they are made with slightly stale or hard cheese. Cheddar's creamy texture is ideal for these scones but several other types of cheese are suitable, such as Lancashire or Red Leicester which have equally strong flavours.

Chocolate & Mint Fudge Cake

INGREDIENTS

6-10 mint leaves
175g/6oz/¾ cup caster sugar
115g/4oz/½ cup butter, plus extra
for greasing
75g/3oz/½ cup freshly made mashed potato
50g/2oz plain chocolate, melted
175g/6oz/1½ cups self-raising flour
pinch of salt
2 eggs, beaten
FILLING
4 mint leaves
115g/4oz/½ cup butter
115g/4oz/¾ cup icing sugar
30ml/2 tbsp chocolate mint liqueur
FUDGE TOPPING
225g/8oz/1 cup butter
50g/2oz/¼ cup granulated sugar
30ml/2 tbsp chocolate mint liqueur
30ml/2 tbsp water
175g/6oz/1¼ cups icing sugar
25g/1oz/¼ cup cocoa powder
pecan nut halves, to decorate

SERVES 8–10

1 Tear the mint leaves into pieces and mix in a bowl with the caster sugar. Leave overnight.

2 Preheat the oven to 200°C/400°F/Gas 6. Grease and line a 20cm/8in cake tin. Sift the mint-flavoured caster sugar, discarding the mint leaves. Cream the butter and mint-flavoured sugar with the mashed potato, then add the melted chocolate. Sift in half the flour with the salt, and add half the beaten eggs. Mix well, then add the remaining flour and eggs to the mixture.

3 Spoon the mixture into the prepared cake tin. Bake for 25–30 minutes or until a skewer inserted in the cake comes out clean. Turn the cake out on a wire rack to cool. When cool, split it into two layers.

4 Make the filling. Chop the mint leaves finely. Cream the butter, then mix in the icing sugar and mint leaves to give a smooth buttercream. Sprinkle the liqueur over both layers of the cake, then sandwich them together with the filling.

5 Make the topping. Mix the butter, granulated sugar, liqueur and water in a small saucepan. Heat until the butter and sugar have melted, then boil the mixture for 5 minutes. Sift the icing sugar and cocoa into a large mixing bowl and add the hot butter and liqueur mixture. Beat with a large spoon, until cool and thick. Cover the cake with the fudge topping and decorate with the pecan nut halves.

Index